Shimmer and Shine

Kitchen Magic

Recipes by Betsy Haley

Illustrated by Marcela Cespedes-Alicea

Walter Foster Jr.

6 Orchard Road, Suite 100
Lake Forest, CA 92630

Printed in Shenzhen, China
10 9 8 7 6 5 4 3 2 1

Table of Contents

Before You Make Your Wish

The kitchen is where different foods combine in a magical way to make delicious dishes. Although it's fun to cook, remember that some things in the kitchen can be dangerous for little hands. Ask an adult for help before starting any of the recipes in this book. To start our magical adventure, gather some cooking supplies and ingredients, and wish up some yummy recipes with Shimmer and Shine!

Ask an adult for help before starting any of the recipes in this book!

Best Friends' Brunch

It was such a beautiful morning in Zahramay Falls that it gave Leah an idea: She and her genies, Shimmer and Shine, should have a Best Friends' Brunch!

"What's a brunch?" Shimmer asked.

"Brunch is a meal that people eat on weekends," Leah explained. "It's a combination of breakfast and lunch!"

"Two meals in one?" Shine asked excitedly. "Leah, I think I love brunch!"

"We'll make a few tasty treats," said Leah, "our friends will, too—and then we'll all share!"

Egg Cups Divine

You'll need an adult to help you with the microwave!

This recipe needs

- 2 eggs
- 2 tablespoons low-fat milk, soy milk, or unsweetened almond milk
- pinch of salt and pepper
- 1 tablespoon shredded cheddar cheese

Serves 1

In the kitchen, Leah found eggs, milk, and cheese. But she wasn't sure what to do with them.

"You could make a wish," Shine suggested.

"That's a great idea," said Leah. "I wish we had a delicious dish to share with our friends!"

Shimmer clapped her hands. "Boom Zahramay, first wish of the day! Shimmer and Shine, Egg Cups Divine!"

With an adult helper, follow these instructions to make Egg Cups Divine at home!

Directions

1. In a microwave-safe mug, whisk together eggs, milk, salt, and pepper.

2. Microwave on high for 45 seconds. Stir.

3. Microwave for another 45 seconds until eggs are firm.

4. Top with cheese and microwave for 15 seconds or until cheese melts.

Pretty Pet Portraits

You'll need an adult to slice the banana and strawberries!

This recipe needs

- toast
- nut butter spread, such as peanut butter, almond butter, or apple butter
- cream cheese
- sliced banana and strawberries
- blueberries

Serves 1

"You can't have eggs without toast," Shine said. But instead of leaving the toast plain, she made it extra special. Shine decorated each piece of toast to look like the faces of their pets: Tala the monkey, Nahal the tiger, and Parisa the fox.

"Like I always say," Shine told her twin sister, "you can never have too many portraits."

"I've never heard you say that before," said Shimmer.

"That's because I just made it up!" Shine giggled.

For Tala's face

Spread nut butter or apple butter into a circle on toast. Cut two banana slices in half to create the ears and mouth. Place two blueberries for the eyes.

For Nahal's face

Spread nut butter or apple butter into a circle on toast. Place two blueberries in the center for eyes. Place two thin strawberry slices (pointed end up) on top for the ears. Create the nose and whiskers by using the tip of a strawberry slice and then cutting the rest of the slice into thin strips.

For Parisa's face

Spread 1 tablespoon cream cheese
on toast. Thinly slice two strawberries.
Place two slices on the top of the toast
to create the ears. Arrange remaining
strawberry slices in a triangle shape.
Place two blueberries for eyes and one
for the tip of the nose.

Brrr-eakfast Sundae

You'll need an adult to help you with the blender.

This recipe needs

- 2 frozen bananas
- ½ cup frozen blueberries or other frozen berries
- ½ cup low-fat milk, soy milk, or unsweetened almond milk
- topping suggestions: shredded coconut, almond butter, fresh fruit

Serves 2

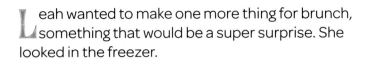

Leah wanted to make one more thing for brunch, something that would be a super surprise. She looked in the freezer.

"If brunch is breakfast and lunch, couldn't we combine breakfast and dessert, too?" wondered Leah.

"Of course!" Shine said. "We can do anything!" She used the breakfast ingredients in front of her and a little bit of magic to make a kind of ice cream.

Leah tasted the cold dessert and said, "Yum!"

"What should we call it?" Shimmer asked.

Leah laughed. "Brrr-eakfast Sundae!"

Directions

1. In a blender, combine frozen bananas, frozen berries, and milk. Blend until smooth.

2. Top with your favorite toppings.

Pizza Pancakes

This recipe needs

- 1 cup flour
- ½ cup cornmeal
- 3 teaspoons baking powder
- 1 teaspoon salt
- 1 cup low-fat milk, soy milk, or unsweetened almond milk
- 2 eggs
- nonstick cooking spray
- 1 cup pizza sauce
- 1 cup shredded mozzarella cheese
- ½ cup mini pepperoni, mushrooms, or any other pizza topping

Serves 10

Zac and his genie, Kaz, arrived carrying a plate topped with something that smelled delicious.

"We brought pizza pancakes!" said Zac.

"Pizza what, now?" asked Shine. "Please tell me I can eat this!"

"Pizza pancakes are 100 percent edible," said Kaz.

"What's a pizza pancake?" Leah asked.

"Oh, just something Kaz cooked up for one of my wishes," said Zac. "It's pizza AND a pancake. The best of both worlds!"

Directions

1. In a medium bowl, whisk together flour, cornmeal, baking powder, salt, milk, and eggs until thoroughly combined. There can be a few lumps.

2. Heat a skillet or griddle over medium heat. Spray with nonstick spray. Ladle ¼ cup of batter per pancake onto the skillet. Cook until bubbles form on the surface, then flip once and cook until golden brown, about 1½ minutes per side.

3. Transfer pancakes to a baking sheet.

4. Preheat broiler.

5. Spread each pancake with 1 tablespoon of pizza sauce. Top with 1 tablespoon shredded mozzarella cheese and mini pepperoni, mushrooms, or other pizza topping.

6. Broil for 2 minutes until cheese melts.

To make pizza pancakes like Zac and Kaz, follow these instructions with your adult helper!

The Many Tastes of Zahramay Falls

"Thanks for teaching us about brunch, Leah," Shimmer said.

"That was Zahramazing!"

"Now it's our turn," Shimmer said. "We're going to show you some

of the awesome things to drink and eat in Zahramay Falls!"

Bela Beach Cooler

Leah and the genies hopped on their magic carpet and headed straight to Bela Beach.

"The beach is so pretty," Leah said.

"And super hot," added Shine.

"That's why you have to have Bela Beach Cooler," explained Shimmer. "It's a tasty way to stay cool!"

Directions

1. Combine all ingredients in a pitcher or punch bowl. Chill before serving.

This recipe needs

- 2 cups orange juice
- 2 cups limeade
- 16-ounce container pomegranate juice
- two 12-ounce cans of soda water

Serves 8-10

Zahramay Zucchini Fries

This recipe needs

- 2 large zucchini, cut into 4-inch-long strips
- ¼ cup flour
- salt and pepper
- 2 cups panko breadcrumbs
- 1 teaspoon garlic powder
- ½ teaspoon cayenne pepper
- 2 eggs
- nonstick cooking spray

Makes 6 servings

After they finished their drinks, Leah, Shimmer, and Shine jumped on their carpet and zoomed to the Genie Market. There were so many colors, sights, and sounds! The merchants at the market sold everything from magic bottles to magic potions! There were stalls with genie jewels, fresh fruits, and flowing fabrics. Anything you ever wanted could be bought at the Genie Market!

"What's that crispy treat?" Leah asked, pointing to long, golden strips on a platter.

"Zahramay Zucchini Fries!" said Shimmer. "You eat them with a creamy dip. We should get some."

"I was hoping you'd say that!" said Shine.

For the dip

- one 5-ounce container low-fat Greek yogurt
- 1 garlic clove, minced
- zest of 1 lemon
- 1 teaspoon lemon juice
- 1 tablespoon fresh dill, finely chopped

Directions

1. Preheat oven to 425 degrees.

2. Pour flour into a large sealed bag. Add a pinch of salt and pepper to season. Add zucchini, seal the bag, and toss until zucchini is fully coated in flour.

3. In a small bowl, stir together panko breadcrumbs, garlic powder, cayenne, ½ teaspoon salt, and ½ teaspoon pepper.

4. In another small bowl, thoroughly whisk eggs.

5. Piece by piece, shake excess flour from zucchini, dip into eggs, allow excess to drip off, and then coat in panko mixture. Place on a baking sheet lined with parchment paper. When all pieces are coated, spray evenly with cooking spray.

6. Bake for 25 minutes until golden brown and crispy.

7. Meanwhile, make the dip. In a small bowl, combine yogurt, minced garlic, lemon zest, lemon juice, and dill. Refrigerate until ready to serve.

You'll need an adult to help you cut and cook the zucchini.

Cheesy Noodle Flowers

This recipe needs

- 1 pound ground beef (or 10-ounce package frozen spinach, thawed and well drained)
- 2 tablespoons olive oil
- 2 cloves garlic, minced
- ⅓ cup onion, diced
- one 28-ounce can crushed tomatoes
- 2 teaspoons Italian seasoning
- salt and pepper
- 12 lasagna noodles
- one 15-ounce container low-fat ricotta cheese
- ¼ cup fresh parsley, chopped
- 1 egg
- 1½ cups shredded mozzarella cheese, divided
- 1 cup Parmesan cheese

Makes 6 servings

"That's why I love eating at the Genie Market," said Shine finishing her fries. "All of the fun, none of the work!"

Hearing Shine's voice, Zeta poked her head out of the magic potions stand. "Ugh, what are they doing here?" she asked her little dragon, Nazboo. "Oh, never mind. Come along, Nazboo. We've got potions to buy!"

Just then, something caught Shimmer's eye at another stall. "Oh, my genie," she said. "You have to try these, Leah!"

On the counter, there was a tray of little swirls that smelled like cheese but looked like flowers.

"What are they?" Leah asked.

"Cheesy Noodle Flowers," Shimmer said. "It has cheese and noodles in the shape of flowers—that's how they get their name!"

"All I know is that they taste genie-tastic," said Shine.

Directions

1. Preheat oven to 375 degrees.

2. Heat a large skillet over medium-high heat. Add olive oil and ground beef. Cook, stirring frequently until meat is fully browned. Remove from heat and drain excess fat.

3. Return to heat and add garlic and onion, stirring until onion softens and becomes fragrant, about 3 minutes.

4. Add crushed tomatoes, Italian seasoning, salt, and pepper. Reduce heat and simmer for 10 minutes.

5. Meanwhile, cook noodles in a pot of boiling water according to package directions. Drain and carefully lay noodles on a baking sheet or large cutting board.

6. In a medium bowl, stir together ricotta, parsley, egg, 1 cup mozzarella, and Parmesan cheese. You could also mash these ingredients together with your hands!

7. Spoon 1 cup of tomato mixture into the bottom of a square baking dish.

8. Spread 2 tablespoons cheese mixture over one noodle. Top with 1 tablespoon tomato sauce. Starting at one end, carefully roll noodle into a spiral shape and place inside baking dish.

9. Repeat for remaining noodles.

10. Evenly top baking dish with remaining sauce and ½ cup mozzarella cheese.

11. Loosely cover with foil and bake for 35 minutes until cheese is melted and sauce is bubbly.

You'll need an adult to help you cut, cook on the stove top, and use the oven.

Gooey Gummy Genie Jelly

This recipe needs

- 1 cup fruit juice
- 2½ tablespoons (3 packets) unflavored gelatin
- 2 tablespoons honey

Makes 30 gummies

"Wow," said Leah as the girls whizzed away from the Genie Market on their carpet. "I can't believe there are so many incredible things to eat in Zahramay Falls!"

"There's even more to explore in Rainbow Zahramay," said Shimmer.

"Really?" said Leah.

"We can go there now," said Shine. "Hang on to your ponytails!"

As the girls flew off, Leah had an idea. "I wish we had a snack for the trip."

"Boom Zahramay! Second wish of the day! Shimmer and Shine, travel snack divine!"

And just like that, some Gooey Gummy Genie Jelly appeared!

The girls flew their carpet until they reached a rainbow-striped river with a big, glimmering, shimmering boat floating on top. It was the Genie Gem Cruiser! They needed it to travel through the rainbow waterfall.

Directions

1. Stir together juice and gelatin in a small saucepan. Heat over medium-low heat, stirring constantly until gelatin fully dissolves. Remove from heat and stir in honey.

2. Carefully pour mixture into candy molds or ice cube trays. Candy molds come in all kinds of shapes, like diamonds, stars, hearts, and more!

3. Refrigerate at least an hour or until fully set.

4. Remove from molds and enjoy.

You'll need an adult to help you with the stove.

31

Rainbow Zahramay

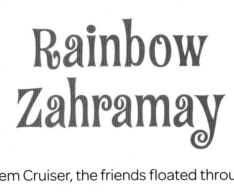

Aboard the Genie Gem Cruiser, the friends floated through the Rainbow Falls. When they came out on the other side, all of their clothes were embellished, and their hair had pretty colored stripes!

"Zahara Zlam!" said Shimmer with a big smile on her face. "I love traveling through waterfalls!"

Fruit Stripe Delight

You'll need an adult to help you with the blender!

This recipe needs

For the red layer:

- ¼ cup chopped beets
- ½ cup sliced strawberries
- ⅓ cup orange juice

For the orange layer:

- ¼ cup carrot juice
- ¼ cup orange juice

For the yellow layer:*

- 1 cup diced pineapple
- ½ a banana
- ½ cup low-fat milk, soy milk, or unsweetened almond milk

For the green layer:

- ½ juice from yellow layer
- 1 handful of spinach

For the purple layer:

- 1 tablespoon sliced beets
- 1 cup blueberries
- ½ a banana
- ½ cup low-fat milk, soy milk, or unsweetened almond milk

*Reserve half of the yellow mixture for green layer

Makes 16 ice pops

F irst stop: the Azar Bazaar, where all the genies in Rainbow Zahramay shopped.

"Look," said Leah, pointing to a vendor. "Those ice pops look like the Rainbow Falls. Zahramazing!"

Directions

1. One at a time, blend together ingredients for each layer until smooth. For the green layer, add a handful of spinach to ½ yellow mixture and blend until smooth. Refrigerate mixtures.

2. Divide red mixture evenly between popsicle molds. Freeze until solid; at least an hour.

3. Repeat for each layer, freezing fully between additions, until molds are full. Freeze overnight.

These ice pops need to freeze overnight, so we will taste them tomorrow!

Beautiful Noodles

Ask an adult to help you prepare the ingredients!

This recipe needs

- 4 cups water
- 2 cups red cabbage, shredded
- one 6-ounce package clear rice noodles
- lemon juice
- toppings, such as veggies, shrimp, sausage, or Parmesan cheese (optional)

Serves 6

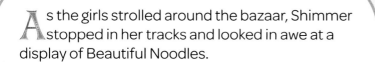As the girls strolled around the bazaar, Shimmer stopped in her tracks and looked in awe at a display of Beautiful Noodles.

"That might be the prettiest food I've ever seen!" said Shimmer.

"And we've seen a lot of food," added Shine.

Directions

1. In a large saucepan, combine water and cabbage. Bring mixture to a boil, then reduce heat and simmer for 10 minutes.

2. Remove from heat. Add rice noodles and soak for at least 10 minutes. The longer the noodles soak, the more colorful they will be. The noodles will turn blue.

3. Drain noodles and divide into serving bowls. Drizzle lemon juice any place you want the color to change. Lemon juice will magically turn the noodles pink!

4. Enjoy with your favorite toppings.

You'll need an adult to help you use the stove top.

Rainbow Pizza

This recipe needs

- nonstick cooking spray
- 1 package refrigerated pizza crust dough
- ½ cup pizza sauce
- 2 cups shredded mozzarella cheese
- ½ cup grape tomatoes, halved
- ½ cup orange bell pepper, thinly sliced
- ½ cup yellow bell pepper, thinly sliced
- ¼ cup broccoli, cut into small florets
- 1 small purple potato, thinly sliced

Serves 4

"I smell something yummy," Leah said as she approached a counter selling Rainbow Pizza.

"And it looks yummy, too!"

The girls got slices and munched on pizza as they made their way back to the Genie Gem Cruiser.

Directions

1. Heat oven to 450 degrees.

2. Spray a 13-inch pizza pan with cooking spray. Stretch dough to cover the pan.

3. Put pizza sauce and mozzarella cheese on top of the dough.

4. Working in a circle, beginning with the crust and working toward the center, place vegetables on top. Begin with a circle of tomatoes on the outside, then orange bell peppers, yellow bell peppers, broccoli, and finally purple potato in the center.

5. Bake 12 to 14 minutes until cheese melts, vegetables are tender, and crust is golden brown.

You'll need an adult to prepare the ingredients and help with the oven.

Tealicious Tea Party

No sooner had the friends returned to Zahramay Falls that a ball
of light swooped in and POOF Princess Samira appeared!

"How would you girls like to come to my palace for a tea party?" she asked.
A little way away, Zeta and Nazboo were returning from the marketplace too.
Zeta spied Leah and the genies from afar and stopped to listen.

"I have a few very special recipes I'd like to share with you,"
Princess Samira said as they headed to her palace.

Teenie Tea Sandwiches

"You hear that, Nazboo?" the tricky sorceress asked her pet dragon. "Very special recipes. I bet she's showing them how to make new potions! If I can get my hands on those potions, I'll be the most powerful person in Zahramay Falls! Let's follow them!"

This recipe needs

- 2 tablespoons butter, softened
- ½ teaspoon lemon zest
- ½ tablespoon fresh herbs, finely chopped
- 8 slices bread, crusts removed
- 1 cucumber, thinly sliced
- 1 tomato, thinly sliced

Serves 4

45

Zeta snuck into the palace and hid behind some cabinets in the kitchen.

"The first recipe I'd like to share requires super special ingredients," Samira explained to the girls.

Zeta was ready to pounce when Samira said, "Very fresh vegetables."

"Vegetables?" the sour sorceress grumbled to her dragon. "That's not a potion!"

Directions

1. In a small bowl, mix together butter, lemon zest, and herbs.

2. Spread 1 tablespoon of butter mixture on a slice of bread. Add cucumbers and tomatoes. Top with another bread slice and cut into four triangles.

You'll need an adult to prepare the ingredients and cut the sandwiches!

Sparkle Cakes

This recipe needs

- 2 cups granulated sugar
- 1¾ cups flour
- ¾ cup unsweetened cocoa powder
- 2 teaspoons baking powder
- 1½ teaspoon baking soda

- 1 teaspoon salt
- ⅔ cup vegetable oil
- 1 cup milk
- 2 eggs, lightly beaten
- 2 teaspoons vanilla extract
- 1 cup hot water

Makes 48 mini cupcakes or 24 standard cupcakes

"The second special recipe needs…" Samira told the girls.

"This is it! Get ready, Nazboo!" Zeta whispered from their hiding place.

"Sparkles!" Samira said as all the ingredients floated out of the cabinets. "You can't make Sparkle Cakes without sparkles."

"Sparkles?" Zeta fumed. "Sparkles won't make me powerful!"

"Cake, yum!" Nazboo said, licking his lips.

For the cupcakes

1. Preheat oven to 350 degrees. Place cupcake liners in a muffin tin.

2. In a large bowl, whisk together sugar, flour, cocoa powder, baking powder, baking soda, and salt.

3. Stir in the vegetable oil and milk. Add eggs and vanilla extract, and stir until thoroughly combined.

4. Slowly and carefully stir in the hot water. Continue stirring until mixture is an even texture.

5. Fill cupcake liners two-thirds full. Bake for 18 to 22 minutes until a toothpick inserted comes out clean. Cool completely before frosting.

For the frosting

- 1 cup butter, softened
- 2 to 3 cups powdered sugar, sifted
- 1½ cups whole raspberries
- ¼ teaspoon raspberry extract (optional)
- edible glitter, sprinkles, fresh raspberries for decoration

You'll need an adult to help you with the blender and mixer.

Directions

1. Purée the raspberries in a blender or food processor.

2. Run puréed raspberries through a fine mesh strainer. You should have ½ cup of strained purée when done.

3. With a mixer, cream butter on medium speed until light and fluffy. Slowly add 2 cups powdered sugar. Add raspberry purée. If the mixture is too watery, add powdered sugar until thick enough to spread. For more raspberry flavor, add raspberry extract (optional).

4. Pipe or spread frosting onto cooled cupcakes. Decorate with edible glitter, sprinkles, or fresh raspberries.

Sweet & Spicy Cinnamon Tea

This recipe needs

- 1 cup water
- 1 teaspoon sugar
- 1 cinnamon stick

Serves 1

For the last special recipe, Princess Samira conjured hot water in a pretty pot. From her hiding place, Zeta watched steam rise from the potion and the air fill with a warm, sweet, spicy smell. She could no longer contain herself!

"Aha!" the sorceress shrieked, leaping from her hiding place and grabbing the pot. "I know you're making a potion, and now it's mine! Ow, that's hot. Whatever. So what does it do? Move mountains? Freeze rivers? Make everyone extra tiny? Hurry up! I can't wait all day to be the most powerful person in Zahramay Falls!"

"It's tea," said Shimmer.

"You hear that, Nazboo! It's..." Defeated, she handed the teapot back to Samira. "Tea."

"And Sparkle Cakes!" said the dragon, eyeing the tray of treats.

"We're having a tea party," Princess Samira said. "Help yourself to a Sparkle Cake, Nazboo! You're both welcome to join us."

"Well, maybe just for one cup of tea," Zeta said, sitting at the table.

Directions

1. Combine water and sugar in a microwave-safe mug. Microwave on high for 2 minutes. Stir to fully dissolve sugar.
2. Add cinnamon stick and steep for 10 minutes.
3. Remove cinnamon stick before drinking.

"Steep" means to soak in hot but not boiling water. Always make tea with an adult helper!

Super Sleepover

After the tea party at Samira's palace, Shimmer, Shine, and Leah made their way home. But instead of going to their bedrooms, they grabbed their sleeping bags. Time for a super sleepover! They set out their sleeping bags, made a pillow fort, and headed to the kitchen to make a snack, dinner, and dessert.

Genie Bling Apple Rings

"I have a recipe for a great snack!" said Shimmer. "I call it Genie Bling Apple Rings!"

"Wait...we're not going to eat jewelry, are we?" asked Shine. "Or are we going to wear our food?"

"No, the *rings* are apple slices, and the *bling* is the yummy stuff sprinkled on top!" said Shine.

Directions

1. Use a knife or apple corer to remove the stem and core from apple.

2. Slice apple into four rings.

3. Spread each slice with ½ tablespoon nut butter or apple butter. Top with ¼ tablespoon toppings of your choice.

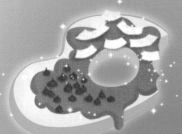

You'll need an adult to help you cut the fruit!

This recipe needs

- 1 apple
- 2 tablespoons nut butter or apple butter
- 1 tablespoon toppings (chopped nuts, sliced fruit, sprinkles, coconut flakes)

Serves 1

55

Fish Stick Tacos

This recipe needs

- one 14-ounce box frozen fish sticks
- ½ teaspoon chili powder
- ½ teaspoon cumin
- one 5-ounce container low-fat Greek yogurt
- ½ cup cilantro, finely chopped
- juice from 1 lime
- 1 teaspoon hot sauce
- salt and pepper
- 5 cups shredded cabbage
- 8 corn tortillas
- sliced avocado and salsa for garnish

Serves 8

The girls looked around the kitchen for something for dinner. There were so many different foods, they weren't sure where to begin.

"I wish we could make something new from the ingredients we already have!" said Leah.

Shimmer clapped her hands. "Boom Zahramay, third wish of the day! Shimmer and Shine, new food combination divine."

"What are they?" Leah asked.

"Fish stick tacos," Shimmer said.

"Wow, I've never heard of that before," said Leah as she took a bite, "but they're delicious!"

Directions

1. Preheat oven according to the fish stick package instructions.

2. Spread fish sticks on a baking sheet and sprinkle with chili powder and cumin. Cook according to package instructions.

3. Meanwhile, in a medium bowl, whisk together yogurt, cilantro, lime juice, and hot sauce. Add salt and pepper to taste.

4. Add cabbage to yogurt mixture and toss until fully coated.

5. Warm tortillas in a skillet over low heat.

6. Place three fish sticks on each tortilla, and add some of the cabbage mixture on top. Top with sliced avocado and salsa.

You'll need an adult to help you with the oven and stove.

58

Cutie Pies

You'll need an adult to help you prepare the ingredients!

This recipe needs

- 1½ cups flour
- ½ teaspoon salt
- ½ cup cold butter cut into small pieces
- 4 to 5 tablespoons ice water
- 4 cups fruit, diced small
- juice from 1 lemon
- ¼ cup granulated sugar
- 1 tablespoon cornstarch
- nonstick cooking spray

Makes 24

After dinner, Shimmer made tiny pies for dessert. The girls then sat in their sleeping bags and ate them.

"These are Zahramazing!" said Leah. "What do you call them?"

"I've never given them a name," said Shimmer.

Just then, Parisa jumped in Leah's lap. She stroked her pet fox's ears. "Parisa, you're such a cutie pie!"

"I know," said Shine. "We can call them Cutie Pies!"

"You hear that, Parisa," said Leah. "You have your very own dessert!"

You'll need an adult to help you with the blender and oven.

Directions

1. Combine flour and salt in a large bowl. Using a pastry blender, cut in cold butter until mixture resembles a course meal. Add ice water, a tablespoon at a time, until dough begins to hold together in a ball. Wrap dough in plastic wrap and refrigerate for at least an hour.

2. In a large bowl, combine fruit, lemon juice, granulated sugar, and cornstarch. Mix thoroughly. Set aside.

3. Preheat oven to 450 degrees.

4. Roll pie dough into a ¼-inch-thick rectangle. Using a 3-inch round cookie cutter, cut out 24 circles.

5. Coat a mini muffin pan with cooking spray. Press a circle of dough into each well of the muffin pan. Allow overlap on the top, as the crust will shrink. Fill each crust with 1 tablespoon of fruit filling.

6. Bake for 25 minutes until crust is golden and filling is bubbling.

The three best friends enjoyed their food, played games, and then got ready to go to sleep.

"What a genie-riffic slumber party!" said Shimmer.

"And a genie-riffic day," added Leah. "I wish we could cook magical food in the kitchen every day!"

"You're out of wishes, Leah," Shine laughed. "But I think we can manage it!"

The End